Anonymous

The Illinois Building and Exhibits therein at the World's Columbian

Exposition

At the World's Columbian

Anonymous

The Illinois Building and Exhibits therein at the World's Columbian Exposition
At the World's Columbian

ISBN/EAN: 9783744718820

Printed in Europe, USA, Canada, Australia, Japan

Cover: Foto ©ninafisch / pixelio.de

More available books at **www.hansebooks.com**

THE...ILLINOIS BUILDING

AND

..EXHIBITS.THEREIN..

AT THE

WORLD'S COLUMBIAN
EXPOSITION
1893

JOHN MORRIS COMPANY
CHICAGO

Illinois Board of World's Fair Commissioners

President...
LAFAYETTE FUNK, Shirley

Vice-president...
DAVID GORE, Carlinville

Secretary...
W. C. GARRARD, Springfield

COMMISSIONERS

J. IRVING PEARCE, Chicago
JOHN P. REYNOLDS, Chicago
J. HARLEY BRADLEY, Chicago
WILLIAM STEWART, Chicago
BYRON F. WYMAN, Sycamore
A. B. HOSTETTER, Mt. Carroll
SAMUEL DYSART, Franklin Grove
W. D. STRYKER, Plainfield
JOHN VIRGIN, Fairbury
E. B. DAVID, Aledo   D. W. VITTUM, Canton
W. H. FULKERSON, Jerseyville
J. W. JUDY, Tallula
LAFAYETTE FUNK, Shirley
S. W. JOHNS, Decatur
E. E. CHESTER, Champaign
JAMES K. DICKIRSON, Lawrenceville
DAVID GORE, Carlinville
EDWARD C. PACE, Ashley
B. PULLEN, Centralia
J. M. WASHBURN, Marion

INTRODUCTORY.

THIS volume has been prepared by order of the Illinois Board of World's Fair Commissioners to serve partly as an index or guide to the exhibits in the Illinois State Building, which were authorized by the State government and partly as an interesting souvenir of the great Columbian Exposition.

The entire cost of preparation, installation and administration by the Commissioners is paid from the State treasury under an Act of the General Assembly, approved by Hon. Joseph W. Fifer, Governor, June 17, 1891.

It is not to any extent a catalogue of the material presented in the several exhibits, nor a report of the labors of the Commission in the discharge of the duties imposed upon its members. Such report, financial and otherwise, as is required by law, cannot be prepared with necessary fullness of historical detail until the great Columbian Exposition with all its realistic magnificence shall itself have become a thing of the past.

The references to the exhibits illustrated are all restricted to the briefest possible mention of the main purpose and character of each.

The State Institutions, which from their nature are debarred from exhibiting, including penal and reformatory, are represented by exterior and interior views of their buildings and grounds.

The Illinois State Building occupies a very conspicuous position in the north part of the park. It was constructed upon plans and specifications approved by the Illinois Board of World's Fair Commissioners, and by the Construction Department of the World's Columbian Exposition Company.

BUREAU OF INFORMATION.

This department consists of four rooms in the northwest gallery, which are fitted up for the convenience and accommodation of all visitors who are actively connected with newspaper journalism. The conduct of the bureau is in charge of the secretary of the National Editorial Association and of the Illinois Press Association, who has an extensive acquaintance among newspaper men, and is looking after their interests in connection with their regular duties as journalists. *The rooms are free to all* and are supplied with easy chairs for resting, and an editorial room fitted up with writing material and desks. A stenographer is also in this room for the convenience of editors, an d such service is free to those requiring it.

SOUTH FRONT ILLINOIS BUILDING.

RELIEF MAP OF THE STATE OF ILLINOIS,

COMPILED BY THE

Illinois Board of World's Fair Commissioners, from a survey of the State made under their direction for this especial purpose in 1892.

SYNOPSIS OF DATA USED AND WHENCE DERIVED.

From the Mississippi River Commission, a line of levels from Cairo to Dunleith; a line of levels from Fulton to Chicago, along the Chicago, Milwaukee & St. Paul R. R.; a series of topographic charts of the Illinois shore of the Mississippi, and the low water slope of the Mississippi.

From the lake survey, a series of geodetic stations between Chicago and Olney.

From the Illinois and Michigan Canal, low water levels of the Illinois River.

From the U. S. Geologic Survey, a series of topographic charts between Chicago and Peoria.

From the coast and geodetic survey, a line of levels from Olney to St. Louis; a line from Centralia to Cairo; and low water levels of the Ohio and Wabash Rivers.

From the U. S. engineers, the preliminary survey of the Hennepin Canal.

From the railroads, profiles of their lines.

Barometric profiles made with moving and stationary barometers, of such railroads as had no profiles.

The bench marks of the lines of levels and geodetic stations were connected with the nearest railroads, and were used to correct the profiles of such railroads.

The elevations above low water of the railroad bridges over the Illinois and Mississippi Rivers were obtained, and the railroad profiles checked by them.

The exact relations of the railroads at intersecting points were ascertained, and the profiles of the roads checked on each other, using those that had been corrected by U. S. data as master systems.

To the outline so established, the details of surface were added by traverses, with barometer and hand level, arranged to intersect railroads as often as possible, and practically to bring the observer within sight of every section of land in his district. Prominent points, either of elevation or depression, were visited, and observations made upon them. Many cross checks and other means of correction were applied to overcome errors in atmospheric pressure, instrumental irregularities, and errors of observation.

Finally, the results obtained were expressed in contour lines on the maps.

Much pains have been taken to make the maps more correct in their horizontal features than any heretofore published. The locations of towns and courses of streams have, in most cases, been either verified or corrected.

The time allowed for the field work was one year, and the total expenditure $15,000. The area covered was 56,000 square miles. It is hoped that future observations will show that the work has been as well done as the limitations of time and funds would admit.

TABLE OF ELEVATIONS above the level of the ocean for each county town, the point of observation in each case being the courthouse, except as noted.

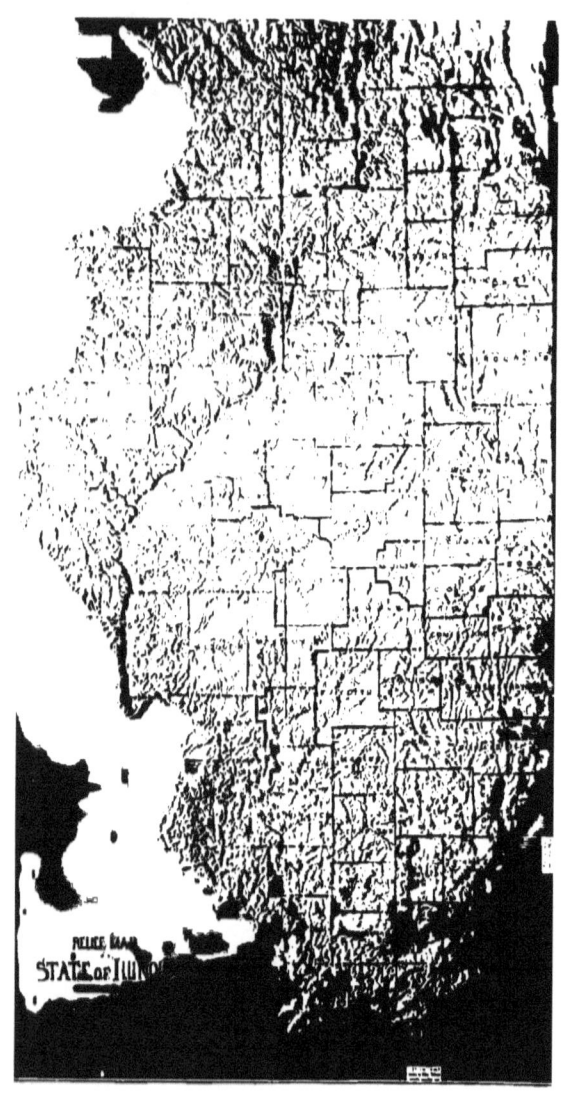

RELIEF MAP OF ILLINOIS.

THE LIBRARY
OF THE
UNIVERSITY OF ILLINOIS

PICTURE ON WALL OF AGRICULTURAL EXHIBIT.
Made of grains and grasses, representing a typical Illinois farm.

OF THE
UNIVERSITY OF ILLINOIS

AGRICULTURAL EXHIBIT.

AGRICULTURAL EXHIBIT.

AGRICULTURE.

The scope and purpose of this department of the State exhibit are described in the law as follows: "A full and complete collection of all the cultivated products in the several branches of agriculture—farm culture, horticulture and floriculture—in illustration of the widely different conditions of soil and climate under which rural husbandry is practiced in the various sections of the State." With a domain extending 387 miles in a north and south line, there is a range of climate which enables Illinois to produce cereals, grasses, vegetables and fruits in the greatest variety and profusion.

In the installation of this department the section representing "farm culture" was organized as distinct from "horticulture and floriculture," the last two being placed together and forming one section. The two sections occupy equal areas at the west end of the main exposition hall.

FARM CULTURE.

The products shown represent:

1. Well selected samples of the crop of 1892 and 1893 in all varieties of grains and grasses, seeds and vegetables, grown in every county of the State, consisting of 100 varieties of wheat, seventy of corn, sixty of oats, besides rye, barley, flax, hemp, broom corn, sorghum, tobacco, cotton, castor beans, peanuts, grass and vegetable seeds; also 120 varieties of native and cultivated grasses.

2. Samples of thirty-three non-alcoholic, commercial, distinct manufactured products of Indian corn, embracing several varieties of sugar, starch, syrups, oils, gums, etc.

This entire collection of farm products is installed in a thoroughly systematic manner, with lavish artistic decoration and tasteful, intelligent arrangement of material throughout, and is located in the northwest corner of the building.

The three sections under the balcony represent the northern central and southern divisions of the agricultural interests of the State. The west tier of shelves contains 160 bottles of beans, peas, flax, red, white and alsike clover, timothy, blue-grass, millet, sun-flower, red-top, Hungarian, yellow oat grass, barley, etc. The second tier of shelves represents the wheat-growing division in 600 bottles correctly labeled, showing the kind and where raised. The third tier of shelves represents the corn-growing districts with 287 bottles showing the different kinds of corn. The fourth tier of shelves contains 500 bottles correctly labeled, showing the kind and quality of oats raised in the State.

The above named exhibits, taken together with the decorations of the balcony, show the agricultural interests of the State which produces annually 30,000,000 bushels of wheat, 230,000,-000 bushels of corn, and 111,000,000 bushels of oats.

Just north of the balcony is the pagoda, decorated with grasses and grains, showing what is grown and what can be done in the way of decorations with agricultural products.

Along the north wall, in glass cases, are all the different kinds of native and cultivated grasses, correctly labeled.

On the west wall is a farm scene, representing a model Illinois farm. This picture, 24x32 feet, with a four-foot frame, is made entirely of grasses and grains in their natural colors, under the direction and supervision of the Agricultural Committee of the Illinois Board of World's Fair Commissioners; more than one-half the work being done by Illinois girls. The time consumed in making the picture would equal the work of one person 480 days.

There are also shown samples of all matured crops of grains, grasses and vegetables of 1893, which are collected and placed on the tables as the season of maturity progresses from south to north through the entire length of the State, nearly 400 miles.

GRAIN INSPECTION AND FORESTRY EXHIBIT.

THE LIBRARY
OF THE
UNIVERSITY OF ILLINOIS

DEPARTMENT OF FORESTRY.

This department was created less than nine months before the Fair was opened to the public, and on that account the display in point of variety is not as complete as it would have been had more time been allowed to secure the rarer kinds, and the display of cultivated woods has suffered more or less from the same cause.

Notwithstanding the short time in which the collection had to be made, the department contains ninety-one specimens of indigenous trees, seventy-three of which represent species of the highest commercial value.

In the domain of cultivated timber, great progress has been made by our farmers, and yet, with ample material at hand, it was not altogether an easy matter to secure specimens. The fact is that there are few cultivated trees but what have been grown for some specific purpose, and consequently, instances were rare where our tree planters were willing to part with the reward of years of labor, just developing into perfection. This circumstance, together with lack of time for more extended research, will account for the absence of many varieties known to be in successful cultivation in our State. It is a pleasure, however, to record the fact that of the seventy-three specimens now on exhibition, not one was relinquished for gain; and, therefore, each piece so furnished, testifies to the general appreciation of the aims and purposes of our State exhibit, and a devotion to the success of the great Exposition itself.

It is not too much to say that the specimens shown, and with these the unique exhibit of the farm wagon of many woods, comprise object lessons of rare interest to every farmer, planter and land owner in the West. All of the varieties shown of cultivated trees can be grown with equal success in all parts of our State; besides which there are several others that are to-day successfully cultivated south of the thirty-ninth parallel of latitude, south as the southern catalpa, cypress, and others, of which no specimens were available within the brief space of time allotted.

Nothwithstanding this, it is safe to say that there is no State collection of a similar nature within the limits of the Exposition that equals the Forestry Exhibit of the State of Illinois.

RAILROAD AND WAREHOUSE COMMISSION, DEPARTMENT OF GRAIN INSPECTION.

This exhibit shows the complete process of grain grading and inspection; the system of recording the inspection and the issuing of certificates thereon; the warehousing of the grain after inspected; the registration, shipment and clearance of the same; and practically exemplifies the every-day routine of the work of the inspection department. Samples of all the commercial grades of grain, and such of the fancy grades as ever find their way to this market, are shown. To those who may desire it, samples of any particular kind or grade of grain are presented.

HORTICULTURAL EXHIBIT.

THE LIBRARY
OF THE
UNIVERSITY OF ILLINOIS

HORTICULTURE AND FLORICULTURE.

The products exposed in this section represent:

1. The fruit crop of 1892, chiefly apples, which were held in cold storage until the opening of the Exposition, May 1, 1893.

2. Samples of all fruits cultivated in this State, from the Ohio River to the Wisconsin line, in succession as the season of maturity advances from south to north. With the exception of apples, in which a partial failure was unavoidable, the display fairly reflects the capability of every section of the State for the production of fruit.

These samples have included during the season 42 varieties of strawberries, exhibited from May 10 to July 30; 28 varieties of raspberries from June 1 to August 9; 26 varieties of blackberries from June 16 to August 10; cherries in 23 varieties from May 28 to August 16; gooseberries in 22 varieties from May 26 to August 18; currants in 18 varieties from June 1 to August 12; grapes in 36 varieties from July 4, and being continued; plums in 22 varieties from June 24, and being continued; apricots in 6 varieties from July 12 to August 20; peaches in 38 varieties from June 10, and being continued; pears in 36 varieties from June 24, and being continued.

Notwithstanding the exceptionally unfavorable season for apples, there have been exhibited 18 varieties of summer apples, 22 varieties of fall apples, and 46 varieties of winter apples.

In addition to above there has been constantly on exhibition quite a quantity of miscellaneous and unnamed fruits.

At the date of preparing this outline the exhibit is by no means complete; numerous varieties of the later fruits having not been received for the year 1893.

3. A large display of choice, cultivated flowers, indigenous and exotic, and ornamental plants.

Owing to want of time for preparation and the fatal delays

incident to the transportation of cultivated delicate flowers and plants, it was entirely impracticable to obtain any considerable display of these from remote parts of the State. As it is, the Floricultural section, with its lavish profusion of the choicest material and beautiful arrangement combines admirably with the pomological section to which it is so naturally and closely allied.

The entire section has been, and will continue to be, subject to daily changes of products throughout the entire term of the Exposition.

CULTIVATED TIMBER AND FISH EXHIBIT.

STATE FISH COMMISSION EXHIBIT.

When the act creating the Illinois State Board of World's Fair Commissioners was passed, and an appropriation made to enable them to adequately display the resources of the State, an item directing the Illinois State Fish Commission to make an exhibit of the fishes of Illinois to illustrate the work of the commission was included.

A number of consultations were had between the Board of Illinois World's Fair Commissioners and the Fish Commissioners as to the best mode of making such exhibit. Direct supervision of this matter was turned over to the committee on Natural History, and after a thorough canvass of the whole matter it was decided to depart from the beaten path heretofore followed in making a live fish display, and to undertake to show fish under conditions as nearly natural as possible, discarding the use of the aquaria.

With this end in view the secretary of the State Fish Commission was authorized to make such experiments as would lead up to such a plan of exhibit. Plans were suggested and after a thorough canvass by the committee on Natural History they were adopted. A simple bit of nature suggested itself—a hill, over which in broken streams flowed a body of water, falling into a succession of pools, each lower than the preceding one, until the water finally found its way into a larger pool, or miniature lake, and lost itself in a covered and unseen outlet. The work of the architect was perfect, and nature was closely followed in the arrangement of the vine-covered and moss-grown rocks, through which the water dropped in beautiful cascades, and flowing from one pool to another developed as a whole not only a beautiful picture, but one of the most successful aquaria yet devised. These pools were about twelve inches in depth and in their arrangement gave a surface exposure almost equal to the whole floor space allotted for the exhibit. The fish with which the waters of the exhibit were stocked thrived beyond the most sanguine expectations of the projectors and the loss, usually so heavy in the old style aquaria, was materially reduced, demonstrating, beyond any question, the possibility of so caring for fish as to keep them for an unlimited time in perfect health.

The lake water used, which in its natural state is not, for the greater part of the time, clear enough for aquarium purposes, was thoroughly filtered, and said filtering contributed very largely to the success of the exhibit, the water being so clear that every scale on the fishes could be seen perfectly.

The fish used in making this exhibit were such as are annually distributed by the Fish Commission in their regular work, and were taken, or rescued from the drying pools along the rivers. Annually thousands of fish are left in these drying pools by the receding waters, and the work of the commission has been to rescue them by the use of seines, and after sorting out the best and transporting them to inland waters and depositing them therein, the residue were put into the rivers or lakes near where they were taken.

The photographic views surrounding the exhibit give a very clear idea as to the methods used in the work of the Fish Commission.

FISH EXHIBIT.

ARCHÆOLOGY.

RELICS OF THE STONE AGE.

To the theoretic student who is inclined to speculate on the hidden mysteries of the past, we offer a wide field in our Archæological collection. That a wonderful and intelligent race peopled this country prior to the advent of the red man is abundantly attested, but that they should have passed away without some distinct record of their origin and history is truly remarkable. The dumb relics alone testify to their existence and is the only history of a once numerous and intelligent people.

The advancement of Illinois as the leading agricultural State in the Union, with all the improvements of modern machinery, has been so remarkable, that in the great display of our progress it is naturally suggested to compare the age of steel with the stone age. It is not generally known that the rich fields of Illinois were in ancient times, may be thousands of years ago, inhabited by a primitive people, who subsisted largely by agriculture, and who had the skill to make implements of stone that will be a surprise to many who behold them. These are spades and hoes and various agricultural tools, some of which even resemble old-fashioned plows, that are skillfully chipped from flint; besides there are axes, hammers and other tools of stone and even of iron ore, that besides their weapons and implements of the chase are simply wonderful as showing not only the skill and ingenuity of manufacture, but that the region of Illinois, even in the olden time, was the leading locality of the primitive people of North America. In Illinois were the largest mounds in the United States, as is shown in the photographs and reproductions of the great Cohokia Group in Madison County, near East St. Louis. The center mound of this group is over 100 feet high and covers sixteen acres of ground.

In our exhibit are 100 pieces of pottery from this region showing their skill in the ceramic art. Our Archæological exhibit will be an invaluable collection for the student to learn something not only of the primitive history of our State's first inhabitants, but of general Ethnology.

CASE No. 1.—A representative exhibit of the *flint tools* of the stone age. Each specimen has printed or written on it the locality where found.

CASE No. 2 contains a series of (*a*) *discoidals, or excavated discs;* (*b*) *a series of paddle shaped stone implements of fine workmanship;* (*c*) collection of *ancient ceremonial pipes taken from mounds;* (*d*) fine *ceremonial or banner stones.* Some of these are of quartzite and perforated. For what purpose they were used is unknown.

CASE No. 3.—This case contains a fine representation of the *axes and hammer tools* of the stone age.

CASE No. 4 contains a representative collection of the *ancient agricultural implements* of the stone age, or *stone tools used in digging.*

CASE No. 5 contains, besides three large and fine *mound pipes,* (*a*) a *series of ornaments of shell and copper.*

This case also contains a number of (*b*) *rare copper objects from the mounds: copper axes, needles, breastplates and gorgets.* There is also a number of *bone implements* and some *calcined corn* taken from a mound.

CASE No. 6—This case is similar to No. 1, being a fine representation of the ancient *flint tools* found in Illinois.

In this collection is a unique and very odd-shaped lot of flints from Calhoun county.

CASE No. 7.—The objects in this very prettily arranged case, which is fastened to the wall, form a private collection of flints loaned by Mr. J. C. Converse of Sandwich, Ill.

CASE No. 8.—This large case against the wall contains about 100 pieces of *ancient mound pottery* taken from mounds in Illinois.

FLOOR CASES.

1. Clays, sands, cements and geological sections across the State of Illinois.
2. Soils, rocks and geological section across the State of Illinois.
3. Stratified rocks and fish remains.
4. Stratified rocks, geodes and geodized fossils.
5. (East side) crustacea, insecta, cephalopoda, (west side) saomellibranchiata, pteropoda.
6. (East side) cephalopoda, (west side) gasteropoda.
7. (East side) brachiopoda, (west side) crinoidea, cystidea, echinaidea, blastoideæ.
8. Brachiopoda and bryozoa.
9. (East side) crinoidea, (west side) spongia and corals.
10. Crinoidea and corals.
11 and 12. Plantæ.
13. Sithographic stone from Illinois with samples of work: lead, zinc and iron ores with associated minerals and collection illustrating azoic and sedimentary rocks found in glacial deposits in Illinois. A part of this collection is upon a stand just east of this case.
14. Lithographic stone from Illinois with samples of work.

On wall south of cases 6, 8 and 10 are "cores" from diamond drill borings in Illinois.

On floor north of cases 5 and 7, building stone and coal.

DEPARTMENTS OF GEOLOGY AND ARCHAEOLOGY.

THE LIBRARY
OF THE
UNIVERSITY OF ILLINOIS

DEPARTMENT OF GEOLOGY.

THE LIBRARY
OF THE
UNIVERSITY OF ILLINOIS

GEOLOGICAL DEPARTMENT.

This department is arranged with a view of presenting, in a comprehensive manner, the geological structures of the State and our natural resources in soils, rocks, coals, ores and other like materials of importance to our industries. It comprises maps, diagrams and collections of all the stratigraphical elements of the earth's crust within the boundaries of the State, from the surface down to the bottom of our coal shafts and artesian wells, with a nearly complete series of all the fossil species of animals and plants hitherto discovered in our rocks, and a selection of materials of economical interest.

A large portion of these collections has been supplied by the Illinois State Museum of Natural History in Springfield. Much has been added by special work done since the spring of last year under the direction of the State Geologist, co-operating with the Board.

It is well known that Illinois has an abundance of rich agricultural *soils*, and some less good; but the exact properties of these various soils has never before been investigated, nor have the respective areas of their distribution been defined until now.

Maps prepared and on exhibition, together with samples of soils, will give a very correct idea of their location, and can not fail to be of great importance to the agricultural interests of the State.

In the production of *limestone* for building purposes Illinois contributes very nearly one-third as much as all the other States in the Union together. Some of the more important quarries are represented by exhibits of dressed cubes of their stone.

Lithographic stone has hitherto been supplied to the World from one single locality, Solenhofen in Bavaria. But within the last year inexhaustible quarries of such stone have been opened in Alexander County, Ill., and we have on exhibition a large series of engraved stones and transfers from these quarries, showing that this State will be amply able to supply at least our own continent with its need of this commodity.

In *coal* production the State of Pennsylvania stands first in the Union. But of all the coal mined in the United States, outside of Pennsylvania, our own State contributes one-fourth, the actual out-put approximating twenty million tons annually. Some of our more important mines are represented by exhibits inside the building, while some of them have placed on the lawn in front of this building, columns of coal cut in a single piece from top to bottom of the coal seam, to show its full thickness.

Our *clays and shales*, and other materials utilized in the ceramic arts, represent a great variety of quality, and occur in inexhaustible quantity. A selection of them is to be seen among the geological exhibits together with some manufactured articles, illustrating their utilization. A set of fine *faience*, made of Union County materials, is on exhibition.

Illinois has the only *fluor-spar* mine in the United States, and a good display of this valuable mineral is to be seen in the building, together with lead, zinc and iron ores from the same and other mines.

The *Paleontological Department* contains, among other interesting fossils, more than 1,000 types of new species, first made known to the scientific world by descriptions and figures published in the series of reports of the Geological Survey of Illinois.

GLACIAL GEOLOGY OF ILLINOIS.

Until the investigations relating to the great waterway project now in process of construction the glacial geology seems to have been almost entirely overlooked and misunderstood by the representatives of the State, as well as by those of the United States Geological Survey; but the thorough investigations above referred to and those required for the geological and relief maps for the World's Fair, demonstrate that instead of the Illinois Valley being a water-worn valley it is a glacial pathway of first magnitude, and through which four great Canadian glaciers moved in their passage from their Arctic birthplace to the Valley of the Mississippi. This statement is based upon data already collected and shown by the collection relating to the glacial geology of the State and the lake region, by the geological map and the relief map of Illinois, the latter, especially, revealing at one view the glacial conditions which prevailed over nearly the entire area of the State, thousands of years ago, and brought hither in the form of englacial drift, and spread broadcast, through the agency of the various glacial streams entering the Illinois Valley, the material which pre-eminently entitles her to the cognomen of the " Prairie State.''

By far the larger area of the State was glaciated from the east from the great Lake Huron stream, which invaded the State by a series of inferior streams whose aggregate width was about 200 miles, which fact accounts for the dispersion of the material and the broad extent of the prairies of Illinois. The Illinois Valley represents the equilibrium line between the contending glacial streams entering the State. The valley now occupied by Lake Michigan being in a measure obstructed by the northern peninsula of Michigan, the valley of Lake Huron presented the line of least resistance, which was followed in obedience to natural laws.

From the fact of the convergence of the great glacial streams above mentioned from so vast an area into the State, the geologist will find intermingled in her drift a greater variety of bowlders than can be found in an equal area elsewhere. This statement seems fully justified by the collection on exhibition, every specimen of which is represented in the drift of Illinois. The geologist will find in this collection fragments of conglomerate bowlders, in which he will find pebbles and bowlders which are exact duplicates of typical glaciated pebbles and bowlders found in the drift of to-day, and which are of such shape as to preclude the possibility that they were water-worn. He may also trace some of these same conglomerates, which are of unmistakable identity, back to their nativity, over 900 miles away, by a route so sharply defined as to preclude the possibility that they were transported hither by floating ice. He may trace drift copper from Alton back through the Illinois Valley to the west shore of Lake Michigan, and thence along that shore to the copper region of Lake Superior, along a line conspicuous above all others for the distribution of copper. Distinguishing features for all the glacial streams entering Illinois are so clearly demonstrated in our collection as to seem to fully justify the conclusion above indicated.

ILLINOIS CLAY EXHIBIT.

THE LIBRARY
OF THE
UNIVERSITY OF ILLINOIS

THE CLAY EXHIBIT.

The Illinois clay exhibit, as shown by the illustration, consists of a space 21x21 feet. The space is enclosed with a rustic fence made from tile and terra cotta, covered with ferns, vines and flowers. The pyramid which stands in the center of the space is sixteen feet in diameter, octagon in shape, veneered with fine pressed brick of many colors, shapes and sizes, and decorated with tile, terra cotta, lawn vases, window boxes, flower pots, rustics, statuary, etc., with growing plants, vines and flowers. A rule of the National Commission provides that no manufactured goods shall be shown in State buildings. This exhibit is not intended for a display of manufactured goods, but a place built from manufactured clay goods on which to show Illinois clays. Clays of many kinds and qualities in glass jars are placed on the shelves of the pyramid. Among the collection are clays suitable for the manufacturing of paving, common, pressed, ornamental and fire brick; terra cotta of many colors, sewer pipe, fire-proofing, drain tile, pottery, flower pots, rustic statuary, white granite and incostic tiles. Over 80,000 persons are employed yearly in the factories of this State; seven hundred million brick were manufactured in the vicinity of Chicago in 1892, while in other cities in the State millions of building and paving brick of the finest quality were made. We have large terra-cotta works in the State, also sewer-pipe and fire-brick factories. We have five hundred drain-tile factories, many of which are run twelve months each year and are even then unable to supply the demand. There is an unlimited quantity of clay in our State, which for quality will compare favorably with the clays of any State in the Union.

DEPARTMENT OF NATURAL HISTORY AND ARCHÆOLOGY.

This department consists of the following exhibits: Laboratory of natural history, fishery, forestry, geology and achæology. The division known as the laboratory of natural history was prepared under the direction and special supervision of the State Entomologist. It is a most interesting exhibit. The entomological and ornithological as well as the ichthyological exhibits have been pronounced by scientists as superior to any exhibition of the kind heretofore attempted. The whole division will be found very interesting to the student of nature or even the casual observer. The subjoined catalogue will be of material aid to the visitor.

STATE LABORATORY OF NATURAL HISTORY.

ENTOMOLOGICAL EXHIBIT.

1. ILLINOIS INSECTS INJURIOUS TO THE APPLE.—Specimens of one or more stages of the insect, enlarged figures, and work of 176 species.

2. ILLINOIS INSECTS INJURIOUS TO CORN.—Specimens of one or more stages of the insect, enlarged figures, and work of 149 species.

3. ILLINOIS INSECTS INJURIOUS TO WHEAT.—Specimens of one or more stages of the insect, enlarged figures, and work of fifty-seven species.

4. ILLINOIS INSECTS INJURIOUS TO THE STRAWBERRY.—Specimens of one or more stages of the insect, enlarged figures, and work of fifty-one species.

5. COMMON INSECTS OF ILLINOIS.—A collection of about 1,600 species, representing the different orders and families.

6. THE GEOGRAPHICAL DISTRIBUTION OF ILLINOIS BUTTERFLIES shown by a set of specimens of the species: (*a*) Common to Illinois and the Atlantic Slope; (*b*) common to Illinois and the Pacific Slope; (*c*) common to Illinois and Europe; (*d*) found throughout Illinois; (*e*) found in northern Illinois only; (*f*) found in southern Illinois only.

7. INSECT COLLECTION AS FURNISHED BY THE STATE LABORATORY OF NATURAL HISTORY TO ILLINOIS HIGH SCHOOLS.—A collection of about 460 species, representing the different orders and families.

8. INSECTS EATEN BY BIRDS.—A collection showing the species and higher groups of insects that have been found by the Laboratory in the stomachs of birds.

9. INSECTS EATEN BY FISHES.—A collection showing the species and higher groups of insects that have been found by the Laboratory in the stomachs of fishes.

10. FOOD OF INSECTS.—A collection showing the animal and vegetable constituents of the food of insects so far as they have been determined by the Laboratory by a microscopic examination of the stomachs of the insects.

ORNITHOLOGICAL EXHIBIT.

1. A collection of the birds that reside during the winter in northern Illinois.
2. A collection of the winter residents throughout Illinois.
3. A collection of the winter residents of southern Illinois.
4. A collection of the summer residents of southern Illinois.
5. A collection of the summer residents of northern Illinois.
6. A collection of the summer residents throughout Illinois.

7. A collection of the migrants passing through Illinois.
8. A collection of stragglers in Illinois.
9. A collection of the common game birds of Illinois.
10. A group of wild turkeys.
11. A group of prairie hens.
12. A group of American crossbills.
13. A pair of green herons, with nest and eggs.
14. A group of woodpeckers.
15. A collection of the eggs of birds nesting in Illinois.
16. The food of the robin; a collection showing the total food, both animal and vegetable, eaten by the average robin during the part of the year that is spent in Illinois.

ICHTHYOLOGICAL EXHIBIT.

1. A collection of the fishes of Illinois, grouped as perches, paddle-fishes, gar-fishes, bow-fins, sturgeons, suckers, catfishes, minnows and sun-fishes.

EQUIPMENT OF ENTOMOLOGISTS' OFFICE AND INSECTARY.

This equipment is arranged in two rooms, representing an office and insectary respectively. It may be grouped under the following heads:

1. LIBRARY.—Consisting of (*a*) the *books* or *library proper*, represented in this exhibit by a small section of the actual library of the State Laboratory, and by a complete set of the works published by the Laboratory; and of (*b*) the *Library Catalogue*, represented by that portion of the catalogue of the *Entomological* works of the State Laboratory coming under the letters "*a*" to "*di*" inclusive.

2. OFFICE COLLECTION.—Consisting of (*a*) *pinned insects*, in boxes, represented by a few of the boxes of coleoptera and lepidoptera of the actual collection of the State Laboratory; (*b*)

insects in vials, represented by a few racks of the pattern used by the Laboratory.

3. NOTES AND RECORDS.—(a) *Slip Notes* in boxes in case with "office collection;" (b) *accessions catalogue*, and (c) *special catalogue*, on table with "Publications of the Laboratory;" (d) *card indexes* to accession catalogue and species catalogue in drawer of "Library Catalogue" case.

4. APPARATUS FOR COLLECTION AND PRESERVATION OF INSECTS, including implements for (a) ordinary day collecting; (b) night collecting by light; (c) night collecting by sugaring; (d) ordinary mounting by pinning and on paper points; (e) preservation of larvæ in alcohol; (f) preservation of larvæ by inflation; (g) printing of labels for specimens.

5. A set of the common reagents used in entomological work.

6. Apparatus for the measuring, weighing, mixing, etc., of the various reagents used in entomological work.

7. Apparatus used in the microscopic study of insects; including implements used in hardening, sectioning, staining, and mounting microscopic specimens.

8. Implements and materials used in making pen and ink drawings and water color figures of insects.

9. Furniture and implements required in the ordinary clerical work of an office; including desks, type-write, letter press, etc.

10. Breeding cages and jars of various sizes and styles used in studying the life histories of insects.

11. Apparatus used in the propagation of insect diseases.

STATE LABORATORY OF NATURAL HISTORY AND UNIVERSITY OF ILLINOIS, CHAMPAIGN, ILLINOIS.

UNIVERSITY OF ILLINOIS, CHAMPAIGN.

THE LIBRARY
OF THE
UNIVERSITY OF ILLINOIS

EDUCATIONAL EXHIBIT.

UNIVERSITY OF ILLINOIS.

The exhibit by the University of Illinois represents in distinct departments its College of *Agriculture* and *Agricultural Experiment Station;* the colleges of *engineering,* of *science,* and of *literature,* and the department of *art* and *design.* In each case the exhibit illustrates the facilities for and the methods and results of the instruction given. There are pictures and plans of the buildings, farms, experiment grounds, shops, laboratories and museums; specimens of the apparatus used in the teaching of the various sciences and their application to agriculture and the mechanic arts, and of work done by students of all departments.

The College of Engineering occupies the largest space with the showing made from its departments of architecture and of civil, electrical, mechanical and mining engineering. There are plans and models of buildings designed, machinery planned and made, railroad lines surveyed by students, and a large collection of apparatus.

The College of Science occupies the next largest space with its departments of botany, chemistry, geology, psychology and zoology, in each illustrations being given of the laboratory work performed by students, and specimens from the various museums.

The College of Agriculture combines its exhibit with that of the Agricultural Experiment Station, showing samples of the products of the farms and Experiment Station plats, including a large collection from the University's artificial forestry plantation. There are selections from the apparatus used in the veterinary department.

The College of Literature has fewer material things to show, but illustrates its work by a large number of examination papers, essays and theses prepared by the students.

The work done in industrial art and design is shown by many drawings made by students from the objects represented, showing both the nature and the order of the work.

The University of Illinois is situated between the two cities of Champaign and Urbana, 128 miles southward from Chicago. It owes its origin to the grant of land scrip by Congress in 1862 to each State " for the endowment, support and maintenance of at least one college, whose leading object shall be, without excluding other scientific and classical studies, and including military tactics, to teach such branches of learning as are related to agriculture and the mechanic arts * * * * * in order to promote the liberal and practical education of the industrial classes in the several pursuits and professions of life." The State received scrip for 480,000 acres of land. Champaign County and the Illinois Central Railroad made large donations to secure the location. The State Legislature has made appropriations aggregating $879,900. The estimated value of the University property is about $1,372,000.

The University was incorporated in 1867 and opened to students in 1868. It has had 2,944 matriculated students. For the year 1892-93 its enrollment was 714. It has over fifty professors and instructors.

The University is under the control of a Board of Trustees—composed of the Governor of the State, the President of the State Board of Agriculture, and the Superintendent of Public Instruction, *ex officus*, and nine members elected by the people.

The University has colleges of agriculture, with several full courses, aside from special short courses; of engineering, with courses in mechanical, electrical, civil, municipal and architectural engineering, and in architecture; of science, with schools of chemistry and of natural science, each with several distinct courses; of literature, with courses in English and modern languages, in Latin, in classics and in philosophy and pedagogy. There are also schools of military science and of art and design, and a graduate school. A preparatory department is also maintained.

The exhibit by the University is much the largest made by any educational institution in any department of the Exposition.

EXHIBIT, UNIVERSITY OF ILLINOIS, CHAMPAIGN.

THE LIBRARY
OF THE
UNIVERSITY OF ILLINOIS

Its assignment of space is 6,200 square feet. This large space is more than usually filled; perhaps too much so for the best appearance of the exhibit, which has been planned with reference to illustrating the work of the University in its various departments, rather than with the purpose of compelling the attention of those looking for especially showy things.

The exhibit is divided into six general departments, one for each of the four colleges, one for the art department, and a small general exhibit. In each case the attempt has been made to illustrate the facilities for instruction, and the methods and results of instruction.

The College of Agriculture and the Agricultural Experiment Station have a joint exhibit. There are maps and pictures of the farms, experiment plats and buildings; specimens of the products of the fields, and an especially good showing of grains. Horticultural products are represented by casts of fruits. There is a good collection of woods from the artificial forests. The large amount and variety of work done in the botanical and chemical laboratories of the station is indicated by specimens of apparatus and collections, and by charts showing results of work done. There is a well-arranged chemist's table with its outfit, including a number of contrivances invented at the station.

The veterinary department shows a model of the horse, and skeletons of the horse and cow, with collection of drugs used in veterinary medicine.

Because of the nature of the work, and the number of distinct departments, the College of Engineering has the largest exhibit. The aim has been to illustrate both the method of instruction and the character of the work done in the seven technical or professional courses of the college. Photographs and specimens of the equipment of the shops, laboratories, draughting rooms and museums are shown. The exhibit of students' work, comprising drawings, maps, plans, designs, models and shop work, as well as results of original investigation, is large and varied. Courses of study are shown by charts, and the rapid growth in number of students in these courses is shown graphically.

In the department of mechanical engineering machines

ready for operating, apparatus for use in testing steam engines and boilers, and for other purposes in the experiment laboratory; a display of work done by students in the mechanical shops, from ordinary practice pieces to a steam pump; drawings and designs for engines and other machinery, as well as the work of the various theoretical studies of the courses, are shown.

In the exhibit by the department of civil engineering are specimen surveying and astronomical instruments, many volumes of problems, drawings and designs, and a collection of maps, plans and designs in surveying, railroad and road engineering, geodosy, astronomy, bridge design, water supply engineering, etc., from the survey of a farm field to the location of a railroad, and from the design of a sewer to the plan of a long-span bridge.

The architectural exhibit is composed mostly of drawings and designs made by students. Here are drawings of residences and great buildings in the same detail and finish as might be sent out from an architect's office. Models of stairs and shop practice work in carpentry and joinery, turning and cabinet-making form an attractive display. The whole course of study is illustrated.

In mining engineering, a similar line of drawings, photographs and models from assay specimens to mine operation show faithfully the character and methods of the instruction.

The exhibit from the department of physics consists of full sets of apparatus used by students of the sophomore class in studying in the laboratory the most important principles of physics. Accompanying the set of apparatus for each experiment is a note-book of a student showing the original record of his work. Photographs of the cabinets of apparatus used in illustrating lectures and of the lecture room and laboratory are also shown.

The exhibit from the department of electrical engineering consists of a large motor, a large direct current dynamo mounted upon a cradle dynamometer, a water rheostat, various types of storage batteries and sets of apparatus for typical experiments in direct current work. A set of photographs show some of the most important rooms of the electrical engineering laboratory.

The College of Science has the next largest assignment of space. In natural science an attempt is made to show the equipment for students' use in their regular laboratory and classroom work, and to present examples of illustrative material. Of the former there are laboratory desks fitted up with instruments and material, microscopes, dissecting instruments, bottles of stains and reagents, drawing apparatus, etc. There are also shown the results of such work by prepared specimens.

There is an attractive display of mounted mammals and birds, and a wonderful series of dissections in alcohol, together with interesting exhibits of wax models, drawings and charts. On the botanical side is a fully equipped bacteriological table, photomicrographs of wood sections, some of which are greatly enlarged, an herbarium, and cases of apparatus and specimens.

In the geological exhibit is shown a student's outfit of tools and chemicals, microscope, with slides, etc., a series of ornamental stones, and samples of Illinois building stones; samples of the University collection of casts of fossils, and a series of charts illustrating the working of geological forces in different localities.

In the exhibit by the chemical department, a desk, such as is used at the University, is shown, with the fittings, apparatus, chemicals, etc., supplied to students. Sets of chemical preparations, both inorganic and organic, which have been made by students, are exhibited, as illustrating the scope of their work, as well as the care and skill exercised in manipulation. There is also a supplementary set of organic and inorganic substances, not prepared by students, but used together with the other sets in illustration of the subjects then under consideration.

The work in quantitative analysis is represented by sets giving graphic illustration of chemical composition of ordinary substances, such as milk, butter, coal, clay, glass, etc., which have been prepared to correspond with analyses made by students in the ordinary course of work; the students' reports being exhibited with the substances.

Theses prepared by students who are candidates for the degree of Bachelor of Science in Chemistry serve to indicate the student's ability in partially independent work.

The work in the special lines of pharmacy is represented chiefly by preparations made by students in this department.

The exhibit from the College of Literature is necessarily limited in space by the character of the work done by it, since the instruction does not as readily furnish material for exhibition as the technical and scientific colleges. There are thirty-six volumes of examination papers from all the classes taught during the winter term, 1893; twenty-two volumes of essays, orations and translations; nine volumes of graduating theses. Text books are shown as far as necessary to illustrate methods of instruction. There is a collection of periodicals from the library for the use of students; also of the periodical literature of education. Maps and charts illustrating methods of instruction are shown. Large pictures of library, class-rooms, halls of the literary societies, athletic hall, military department, etc., as well as pictures of Greek and Roman architecture, cover the walls.

The exhibit by the department of art shows, by a large number of examples, the work in free-hand drawing done by students from the different departments of the University and also the work of the regular students of art and design. The exhibit is so arranged that the work may be examined in the order in which it is done.

STATE NORMAL UNIVERSITY, NORMAL, ILLINOIS.

THE LIBRARY
OF THE
UNIVERSITY OF ILLINOIS

ILLINOIS STATE NORMAL UNIVERSITY.

LOCATION—First floor, east wing, south of center aisle, and near east door.

COMPOSITION—Four upright cases, lettered from the west, A, B, C, and D, respectively, and the back of the cases of S. I. S. N. U. exhibit. On the latter, outlines of courses of study, of school work, etc., are displayed. A display of bound maps is near these outlines.

CASE A is given up to a display of photographic views of the buildings, exteriors and interiors, and of classes, together with drawings, freehand, perspective and sketching, and color work.

CASE B contains work in geography and the training school. The latter showing grade work.

CASE C shows work in drawing, botany, physics and chemistry.

CASE D is devoted to an exhibit of the work of students in zoology and physiology.

There are five show cases, numbered 1, 2, 3, 4, and 5, respectively.

In case 1 are Christmas souvenirs made by pupils in the training school.

Case 2 contains clay modeling by primary and intermediate pupils.

Case 3 is filled with clay modeling in fruit forms and historic ornament by normal students.

Case 4 shows forms of paper work by normal students.

Case 5 contains apparatus used by teacher and pupils in the science department of the normal.

STATE NORMAL UNIVERSITY, NORMAL.
SOUTHERN NORMAL UNIVERSITY, CARBONDALE.

THE LIBRARY
OF THE
UNIVERSITY OF ILLINOIS

SOUTHERN ILLINOIS STATE NORMAL UNIVERSITY.

An Act of the General Assembly of the State, in 1869, gave birth to this institution. On the 6th day of September, 1874, the regular work of the school commenced.

The object of the school is to do a part of the work of education undertaken by the State. The character of this work is shown under the following heads, viz.: A normal department, including a normal course of study, and the training work; a high school department, and a preparatory department, including a grammar and a primary school.

The normal department gives thorough instruction in the elementary and higher portions of the public-school course of study, and fits students by knowledge and practice for the duties of the teacher. The Training work comprises (1) mental science and pedagogy; (2) regular attendance upon the meetings of the practice teachers for a study of methods of instruction and management of pupils and classes, and (3) actual teaching in the preparatory schools under the direction of the training teachers.

The high school department fits students for college or business.

The preparatory department is designed to give instruction in the common branches of an English education, and to supplement the acquirements of young persons who come from the public schools with a training too imperfect to admit them to the normal school. The course covers eight years—four years in the primary, and four years in the grammar school. In these two schools the student finds an example of what schools below the high school should be. They also afford to those preparing to teach, a place where they may at suitable times practice the calling of the teacher under the supervision of competent training teachers.

The tuition in the normal department is free; in the high school $21 per year; in the preparatory (excepting the first two grades which are free), $10 per year.

THE EXHIBIT.

The exhibit made by the southern Illinois State Normal University at the World's Columbian Exposition is in two general parts, viz. :—Preparatory and normal.

In the preparatory department is represented the work of the eight grades of the common schools.

This part of the exhibit includes work in the branches studied by the children and is shown in bound manuscript volumes, and on charts in cases. On the charts and in the bound volumes is shown work for each month of each year in the eight years' course. In this way the progress of the children is shown as is also the success of the practice teachers in their work of instruction.

In this department, also, are shown charts in reading, language, and number, prepared by the practice teachers under the direction of the training teachers.

That portion of the exhibit made by the normal department is shown in manuscript volumes, and in drawings, illustrations, and outlines, on charts in cases. The manuscripts discuss principles and methods of instruction, and show progress of students by means of monthly or term examinations. The drawings, illustrations and outlines show methods of instruction in the several studies.

A goodly number of photographs of classes, buildings, rooms, apparatus and grounds are shown in the exhibit; also a few of the material objects used in the preparatory department.

The school has at the exhibit for free distribution to those interested in normal work, a hand-book giving much valuable information about the school and its methods.

STATE NORMAL UNIVERSITY, CARBONDALE.

THE LIBRARY
OF THE
UNIVERSITY OF ILLINOIS

PUBLIC FREE SCHOOLS.

In February, 1855, the General Assembly of the State of Illinois passed "An Act to establish and maintain a system of free schools."

The principles upon which our system of Public Instruction is based are: The just moral and intellectual claim of every child in the commonwealth to an education commensurate with the importance and dignity of his obligations and duties as an upright, intelligent and loyal citizen; the corresponding obligation of the State to make adequate provisions for such an education for all; the inseparable relation of universal intelligence and probity to the strength and perpetuity of a republican government.

In the year 1855 the population of the State was 1,306,576; pupils enrolled, 173,531; number of teachers, 5,684; average monthly salary of male teachers, $29.16; of female teachers, $16.43.

In the year 1870 the population was 2,539,801; pupils enrolled, 652,715; number of teachers, 28,081; average monthly salary of male teachers, $48.35; of female teachers, $36.66.

In the year 1890 the population was 3,826,351; pupils enrolled, 778,319; number of teachers, 23,164; average monthly salary of male teachers, $54.63; of female teachers, $44.41.

In the year 1892 the population was ————; pupils enrolled, 809,452; number of teachers, 22,346; average monthly salary of male teachers, $56.92; of female teachers, $46.06.

The public free schools are, for convenience in describing the scope and purpose of the work done, classified into rural, graded and high schools.

The rural schools are those established in country districts, and are designed to furnish elementary and, in a limited degree, secondary instruction.

The graded schools of cities afford elementary instruction, and fit for the high schools.

The high schools furnish secondary instruction, and prepare for the State University and other institutions of higher learning.

This classification has been kept in view in the exhibit of school work and appliances made under direction of The Illinois Board of World's Fair Commissioners.

The exhibit is installed in the northeast part of the Illinois Building upon the main floor. The six cases on the east side of the common school section contain the work from rural schools in the order of grades or years from the first, in front, to the eighth at the back. Thirty-one counties are represented.

The middle cases contain the work from the graded schools of cities arranged in a similar manner. Eighty cities are represented, exclusive of Chicago.

The cases on the west side of the common-school section contain the work from the forty-eight high schools represented.

The quantity of work received is so great that but one sixth can be installed at once. Consequently, work from any particular locality may not be found especially installed, but all is catalogued and carefully arranged so that it can be at once exhibited by attendants, if requested.

The design is to represent the public free school work of the State fully in all phases, and at the same time to preserve the continuity and plan of work in each system of schools.

Each grade should be studied by passing along the aisles parallel to the cases, each system of schools, along the aisles at right angles to the cases.

CITY OF CHICAGO.

On account of the different conditions under which the work is done and the amount of it, the exhibit from the city of Chicago is installed separately from the work from the rest of the State.

It consists of work from the kindergartens, primary and grammar grades, high, manual training and evening schools.

The work embraces about 4,000 mounts upon cards 22x28 inches on wing frames, in cases, and 200 wall mounts under glass in frames.

There are 125 bound volumes representing the work of whole classes of pupils, and selected work, indicating the methods used in presenting different subjects and topics in the various branches.

The work is installed on the north and west aisles, commencing with the kindergartens at the northeast, and progressing to the high and manual training schools on the southwest.

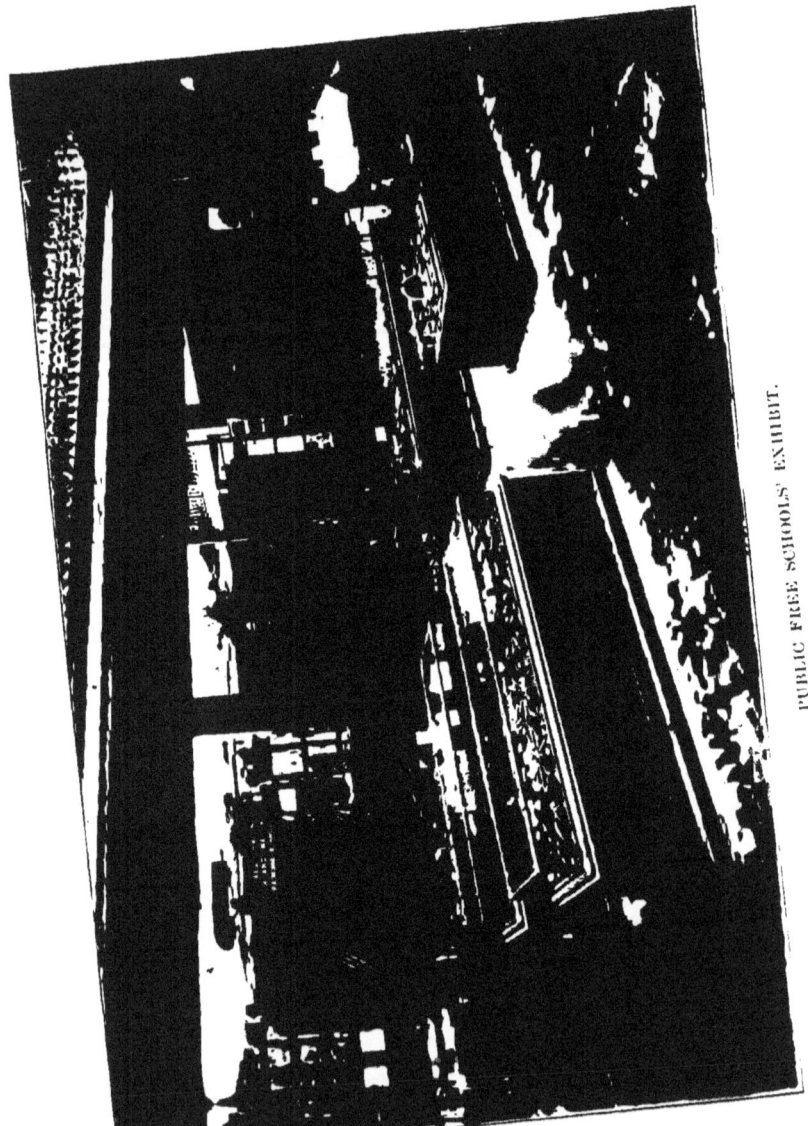

PUBLIC FREE SCHOOLS' EXHIBIT.

THE LIBRARY
OF THE
UNIVERSITY OF ILLINOIS

THE MODEL SCHOOL-ROOM.

The Illinois State Teachers' Association proposed to the World's Fair Commissioners that a suitable school building be erected in Jackson Park, a building sufficiently commodious and equipped in the most approved style to show the educational and hygienic advantages which, under the laws of the State, may be offered to its youth. This building was to contain the eight grades of the primary as well as the four grades of the high-school course, and should besides contain a room to portray the ungraded rural school. This request of the teachers of the State was refused, because the National Commission would not tolerate the erection of buildings below a certain size, and because of the large expense of such structure.

When the Legislature of 1891 made appropriations for the Illinois exhibit, it ordered, among other provisions for showing the educational work of the State, the establishment of a "model common school-room of high grade, fully equipped and furnished under the direction of the State Superintendent of Public Instruction." As soon as the plans for the Illinois building were adopted, the northeast room on the first floor of the building was set apart for this purpose. The room being considerably larger than necessary, it was thought best to partition off enough space so as not to make it too large for actual school-room purposes; this, however could not entirely be effected and so the room is about four feet longer and wider than it need be.

The principle in furnishing the room, however, was not so much to make it a model in size, nor could the contrivances for heating and ventilating be shown, since the Exposition was to be open only during the good season of the year; hence we had to be satisfied to show to the educational public as well as to school officers all that is needed for the well-being and instruction of our youth. The exhibit in the model school-room consists of blackboards, both slate and wood pulp, desks for pupils and teacher, recitation seats, a piano (stout and exceptionally strong for school use), a complete set of geographical maps and of historical charts, a terrestrial and a slated globe, a cyclopedia, an unabridged dictionary, a geographical gazetteer, a library of supplementary reading, physical and physiological apparatus, specimens of stuffed animals and a mineralogical cabinet.

CHARITABLE INSTITUTIONS EXHIBIT.

CARE OF UNFORTUNATES.

A most noticeable and commendable characteristic of a people is their disposition for the relief and comfort of their paupers, lunatics and other unfortunates. While the intentions of the people of the new State were good, it was some years before valuable legislation on this subject was enacted, and it was not until 1839 that advancement in regard to charitable institutions was begun by the State government.

On February 23, 1839, Gov. Thomas Carlin approved a bill passed by the general assembly of that year, establishing the "Illinois Asylum for the Education of the Deaf and Dumb," at Jacksonville, and three years later steps were taken for the purchase of land and the erection of what is now the south wing of the institution, at a cost of $25,000. School opened January 26, 1846, in the building, which was incomplete, by Mr. Thomas Officer, with four pupils, and the term closed with nine. An act of Congress had afforded the people of the State assistance for schools by allowing the sale of the sixteenth section in every Congressional district. In 1837 this fund amounted to $829,815, which the State borrowed at 6 per cent. per annum and the Deaf and Dumb got one twenty-fourth part of the interest up to 1873, which aided the enterprise very materially. After that time, the whole of the interest was made payable to the State Normal University, but the Deaf and Dumb had received $80,000. In 1847 the legislature gave the institution $3,000 which was the first appropriation ever made from the State Treasury for the benefit of any State charity. Since that time its growth has been steady and rapid, and it now stands as the largest institution of the kind in the world.

THE INSANE.

The memorial to the General Assembly of 1846, by Miss Dorothea Lynde Dix, resulted in the establishment of the "Illinois State Hospital for the Insane," at Jacksonville. Funds for starting the institution were not furnished by direct appropriation. A special tax of one-fifth of a mill on the dollar was levied, to be continued for three years, and was increased in 1851 to one-third of a mill, which ran until 1855, when it ceased under the general appropriation act, having brought over $200,000 into the hospital treasury. Meantime expenses in the several counties for support of pauper insane had greatly increased and had to be paid, and the law was changed so that not to exceed $150 annually would be allowed for the support of each inmate after completion of the buildings.

The erection of the center building and two wings at Jacksonville in 1847, had consumed five years and $80,000, being completed under nearly fifty different and independent contracts. Dr. J. M. Higgins, of Griggsville, was the first superintendent, and the first patient was a married woman from McLean County, admitted in 1851.

THE BLIND.

The "Institution for the Education of the Blind" was the third incorporated, which was done in 1849. The State authorized a special tax of one-tenth of a mill for its benefit and this continued until 1855, and in the first two years realized the sum of $90,000 for the new enterprise. The legislature then appropriated $3,000 to enable the trustees to begin the work of building, and a school was opened in April, 1849, by Mr. Samuel Bacon, a blind man from Ohio, who originated the idea of a State institution for the blind in Illinois.

Having thus told of the inception and infancy of the plans for the care of the three principal classes of unfortunates, by State aid, the development of the several institutions, which has placed Illinois prominently before the world in the matter of public charities, may be briefly shown. The act to provide for the appointment of a Board of Commissioners of public charities was recommended by Gov. R. J. Oglesby, passed by the general assembly of 1869, and approved April 9 of that year by Gov. J. M. Palmer. The Rev. F. H. Wines was secretary of the commission from its organization until July 1, 1883, and to him much credit is due for the wonderful success of the board.

NORTHERN HOSPITAL FOR INSANE, ELGIN.

THE LIBRARY
OF THE
UNIVERSITY OF ILLINOIS

NORTHERN HOSPITAL FOR THE INSANE AT ELGIN.

The act establishing this institution was passed by the legislature of 1869; the original building, which is of brick and stone, was completed in 1872, and the present value of the land and buildings is $673,830. The inmates March 31, 1893, numbered males, 557, females, 525, total, 1,082. Average number for last four years, 637. Net cost per capita for the year ending June 30, 1892, $148.62. Net cost per capital per annum average for last four years, $161.88.

THE EASTERN HOSPITAL FOR THE INSANE AT KANKAKEE.

The act creating this institution was passed in 1877, but no appropriation was made for building until 1880. This work was completed in about three years and subsequent additions have followed until the lands and buildings are now valued at $1,393,665 and the institution is the largest of the kind in the world. The inmates March 31, 1893, numbered males, 1,092, females, 921, total, 2013. Average number for the last four years, 1680. The net cost per capita for the year ending June 30, 1892 was $148.26; the net cost per capita per annum for four years, $145.05.

CENTRAL HOSPITAL FOR INSANE, JACKSONVILLE.

The act establishing this hospital was signed in 1846, and the original building, which is of brick, was completed in 1857. The lands and buildings are now valued at $968,626. The number of inmates March 31, 1893, was: Males, 624; females, 585; total, 1209; average number for last four years, 951; net cost of maintaining each inmate last year, $153,42; average net cost per capita per annum for the last four years, $150.86.

SOUTHERN HOSPITAL FOR THE INSANE, AT ANNA.

An act creating this institution was passed in 1869, and bids for buildings were opened April 16, 1870, but ten years elapsed before the completion of the original buildings. The land and buildings are now valued $737,645. On March 31, 1893, the inmates numbered: Males, 511; females, 367; total. 878. The average number for the last four years was 668; the net cost for maintaining them per capita for the last year was $151.65, and average net cost per capita per annum for the last four years, $155.48.

THE DEAF AND DUMB, JACKSONVILLE.

On February 23, 1839, the act for the establishing of the Institution for the Education of the Deaf and Dumb was approved, and the original building, which was of brick, was finally completed in 1857. The buildings are now very extensive, much more so, comparatively, than the small amount of land necessary. The plant is valued at $420,000. The inmates March 31, 1893, were: Males, 290; females, 212; total, 502; average number for last four years, 368.

INSTITUTION FOR THE EDUCATION OF THE BLIND, JACKSONVILLE.

The act for the incorporation of this institution was passed in 1839, and the main building completed in 1854. This was burned in 1869 and immediately rebuilt of brick. The plant is a handsome one and is valued at $213,874. The pupils, on March 31, 1893, numbered: Males, 125; females, 85; total, 210. For the last four years the average attendance was 133. The net cost per capita the last year was $255.36; the net cost per capita per annum for the last four years, $282.93.

ILLINOIS CENTRAL HOSPITAL FOR INSANE, JACKSONVILLE.

THE LIBRARY
OF THE
UNIVERSITY OF ILLINOIS

ILLINOIS SOUTHERN HOSPITAL FOR THE INSANE, ANNA.

THE LIBRARY
OF THE
UNIVERSITY OF ILLINOIS

ILLINOIS' SOUTHERN HOSPITAL FOR THE INSANE ANNEX, ANNA.

THE LIBRARY
OF THE
UNIVERSITY OF ILLINOIS

INSTITUTION FOR THE EDUCATION OF THE DEAF AND DUMB.

THE LIBRARY
OF THE
UNIVERSITY OF ILLINOIS

INSTITUTION FOR THE EDUCATION OF THE BLIND, JACKSONVILLE.

THE LIBRARY
OF THE
UNIVERSITY OF ILLINOIS

ASYLUM FOR FEEBLE MINDED, LINCOLN.

ASYLUM FOR FEEBLE MINDED, LINCOLN.

THE LIBRARY
OF THE
UNIVERSITY OF ILLINOIS

THE INSTITUTION FOR THE FEEBLE MINDED.

Provision for this class of sufferers grew out of the efforts of Dr. P. G. Gillett of the Deaf and Dumb, and Dr. Andrew McFarland, of the Insane, who contended that idiots required a different and separate treatment. In 1865 the General Assembly appropriated $5,000, and a school was opened in the residence of the late Gov. Duncan, at Jacksonville, and was superintended by Dr. Gillett four months free of charge, when it was placed under control of Dr. C. T. Wilbur. In 1871 a bill passed the legislature creating the institution, but no appropriation was made until 1875, when Lincoln was selected as a site and a building was completed in 1877. The lands and buildings are now valued at $255,530. Last year there were 556 pupils : 302 males and 254 females. The average attendance for the four years ending June 30, 1892, was 423. The net cost per capita the last year was $166.46, and the average net cost for the four years per capita per annum was $163.24.

SOLDIERS' AND SAILORS' HOME, QUINCY.

The act creating the Soldiers' Home was approved in 1885, and the buildings, which were made of brick and stone, and on the cottage or detached ward system, were completed in 1888. The land and buildings are valued at $306,800. On March 31, 1893, there were 903 inmates. The average number for the last four years up to June 30, 1892, was 792, and the average net cost per capita per annum for the four years was $161.53, and for the last year, $157.80.

THE SOLDIERS' AND SAILORS' ORPHANS' HOME, AT NORMAL.

In 1865 the home for the orphans of soldiers was incorporated but no appropriation was made. The nine trustees were to receive subscriptions until the sum of $50,000 was secured. But in 1867 the Legislature changed the law, appropriated $50,400 and the home was built at Normal and occupied January 1, 1869. The land and buildings are now valued at $212,550. On March 31, 1893, the children numbered: Males, 235; females, 174; total, 409. For the four years ending June 30, 1892, the average number was 363, who were supported at a net cost of $146.04 per capita per annum, for that time, and for the last year $134.94 per capita.

EYE AND EAR INFIRMARY, CHICAGO.

This institution was started in a small way, many years ago, and was supported by private charity until admitted to control of the State Board of Public Charities, in 1871, when the Legislature made an appropriation for a brick building which was completed in 1874. The property is now valued at $100,120. The patients, March 31, 1893, were 107—males 73 and females 34. For four years ending June 30, 1892, the average number was 134, and the net cost per capita per annum $189.67; net cost for the last year $189.67.

THE STATE REFORMATORY.

The present system of Reform School in Illinois is the result of a move made in 1866 by the State Teachers' Association. One had been started in Chicago by the Rev. D. B. Nichols, in 1855, which ran fifteen years and closed. The Legislature of 1867 passed an act, approved March 5, providing for a Reform School, but no trustees were appointed until 1869, and the school was not opened until 1871. Since then appropriations have been made and the State Reformatory, at Pontiac, for the year ending June 30, 1892, had 324 pupils and for four years prior to that date averaged 346. The net cost per capita per annum was an average of $155.25, and for the last year of that time, $145.89.

SOLDIERS' AND SAILORS' HOME, QUINCY.

THE LIBRARY
OF THE
UNIVERSITY OF ILLINOIS

ILLINOIS SOLDIERS' AND SAILORS' ORPHANS' HOME, NORMAL.

THE LIBRARY
UNIVER

ILLINOIS EYE AND EAR INFIRMARY, CHICAGO.

THE LIBRARY
OF THE
UNIVERSITY OF ILLINOIS

STATE REFORM SCHOOL, PONTIAC.

THE LIBRARY
OF THE
UNIVERSITY OF ILLINOIS

SOLDIERS' AND SAILOR'S HEADQUARTERS'

THE LIBRARY
OF THE
UNIVERSITY OF ILLINOIS

HEADQUARTERS FOR THE SOLDIERS AND SAILORS OF ILLINOIS.

Illinois is justly proud of the part taken by the citizens of the State in the wars of the Union since her admission as a State in 1818.

In the War of the Rebellion her enlistment roll reached the number of 258,217 men—placing her fourth in the list of States and including the "General" of the Union Army, who closed the war by receiving the surrender of the military forces in rebellion.

It was eminently fitting, therefore, that the State of Illinois should provide suitable headquarters for her patriot sons who have seen service, and welcome them at the Columbian Exposition.

In the west end of the State Building a room has been fitted up handsomely for their accommodation. Registers are opened, and at the close will be placed in the archives of the State at the Capitol. The quarters are in charge of a member of the commission in constant attendance, whose duty and pleasure as a "comrade" are to serve the soldiers and sailors of Illinois and of all other States who may honor the commission by calling, and extend to them, one and all, on behalf of the State, a hearty welcome.

JOHN VIRGIN.

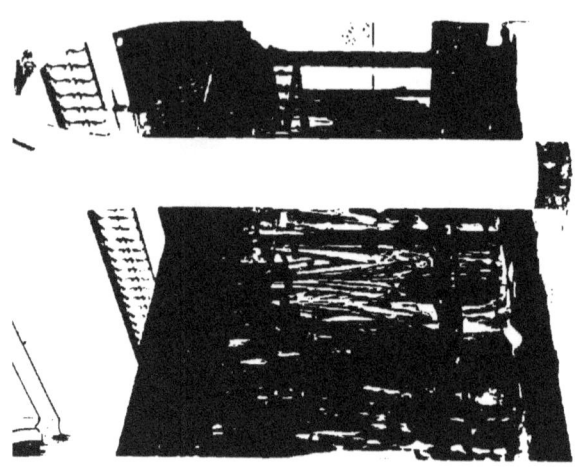

THE LIBRARY
OF THE
UNIVERSITY OF ILLINOIS

MEMORIAL HALL.

Section 4 of the law providing for the participation of the State of Illinois in the World's Columbian Exposition, at Chicago, is as follows:

"Consent of the General Assembly is hereby given that there may be placed on exhibition as part of such collective exhibit, in a suitable fire-proof structure, to be erected for the purpose, such relics and trophies belonging to and in the custody of the State, as the Governor may designate; the same to be and remain at all times during their removal, while on exhibition and during their return to their present depository, in the sole care and charge of their official custodian."

In pursuance thereof, the Illinois Board of World's Fair Commissioners erected Memorial Hall, annexed to the Illinois State Building, and the Governor authorized the Adjutant-General to deposit all of the Illinois battle flags and other relics belonging to the State, in said Hall. The flags are appropriately arranged in large glass cases, and are at all times in the care of efficient custodians.

A roster of the 256,297 Illinois soldiers in the war of the Rebellion, is open to the inspection of all, and thousands of old soldiers, their children and friends, avail themselves of this opportunity of looking over these important records.

Memorial Hall has been during the Columbian Exposition a place of much attraction and interest. It has been visited by a large number of the veterans of the late war who followed those flags, as well as by citizens of all the States and Territories.

The world has seen in these flags an object lesson of patriotism, and a demonstration that the people of the State of Illinois hold in grateful remembrance the deeds of valor typified in these silent but impressive monitors.

THE LIBRARY
OF THE
UNIVERSITY OF ILLINOIS

PENITENTIARIES.

By an act approved February 15, 1827, the Illinois State Penitentiary was located at Alton. One-half the proceeds of the sale of 30,000 acres of saline lands and $10,000 appropriated by the Legislature were given for the site and the erection of buildings. The institution was built of stone, and was first occupied in 1831. On the 19th of February, 1857, an act was passed removing the State Penitentiary from Alton to Joliet. Temporary cells were built as soon as possible, and 200 convicts were taken from Alton to Joliet in 1858. The work of putting up the stone wall and also the buildings was done, principally by the labor of these convicts. The Joliet act appropriated $75,000 and also the proceeds of the sale of the Alton plant. This, however, was but a beginning, as over $1,000,000 have been spent on buildings alone, and the present value of lands and buildings is in the inventory as $1,500,000. The Alton property was sold for $60,000, and in 1860 the last of the convicts were removed to Joliet. The Government later on leased the old property at Alton, and during the War of the Rebellion it was used as a military prison. The real estate of the penitentiary at Joliet is valued at $1,500,000; the average number of convicts for the last year was 1,445; average number for the last four years, 1,391. Cost of maintaining each convict for the last year, $150.60; average cost per annum of each convict for last four years, $152.19.

SOUTHERN ILLINOIS PENITENTIARY.

The location and construction of this institution in southern Illinois was authorized by an act approved February 28, 1867, and the first appropriation was $150,000. Nothing was done under this act, but one which was approved May 24, 1877, located it at Chester, and $200,000 was appropriated for a site and buildings. In 1879 a further sum of $150,000, to complete the penitentiary, and subsequent sums, have brought the amount up to fully $500,000 for buildings, making a total value of lands and buildings of $821,095. Average number of convicts for the last year, 642; average number for the last four years, 663. Average cost of subsistence of each convict for the last year, $212.62; average cost per capita per annum for the last four years, $201.33.

INSANE CRIMINALS.

Provision was made for this class by an act approved June 1 1889, and the asylum located upon the grounds of the southern penitentiary at Chester. Forty-five thousand dollars was appropriated for buildings and $50,000 for furniture and fixtures. Patients are received from the penitentiaries, the insane hospitals and from the courts, where they are acquitted on the ground of insanity. The asylum was opened November 1, 1891, and received three patients at that time. The number on hand June 30, 1892, was 113. On account of the small number during the first part of the time, the expense per capita cannot be fairly estimated. The value of lands and buildings is placed at $46,200.

SOUTHERN ILLINOIS PENITENTIARY, CHESTER.

THE LIBRARY
OF THE
UNIVERSITY OF ILLINOIS

PENITENTIARY FOR INSANE CRIMINALS, CHESTER.

THE LIBRARY
OF THE
UNIVERSITY OF ILLINOIS

PRESENT STATE HOUSE, SPRINGFIELD.

THE LIBRARY
OF THE
UNIVERSITY OF ILLINOIS

SEATS OF GOVERNMENT.

The Constitution of 1818 located the capital at Kaskaskia, to remain until the Legislature should otherwise provide. One session was held there in a rented house and passed an act which was approved March 30, 1819, providing for permanent location. Vandalia was agreed upon and the seat of Government there placed for a term of twenty years from December 20, 1820. The first State house was a wooden structure and cost $3,000. This was destroyed by fire in 1823 and another, made of brick, was erected at a cost of $12,000. By an act approved February 25, 1837, the capital was re-located and Springfield was selected. The act required a bonus of $50,000 and a site of not less than ten acres of land. The place agreed upon by the Commissioners exceeded this amount so that the final cost was $250,000, and the building, though incomplete, was occupied in 1840. This building was made of an excellent quality of stone quarried in Sangamon County. The present State House was begun in 1868 and finally completed in 1886, at a cost of $4,060,000, though the State offices were moved into it in 1876 and the Legislature of 1877 was there held. The State capital building is 399 feet from north to south and 286 feet from east to west. The dome 366 feet high; there are 168 rooms in the building, two passenger and freight elevators, and there are 361 steps from the fourth floor to the top of the dome.

THIRD STATE HOUSE, SPRINGFIELD.

THE LIBRARY
OF THE
UNIVERSITY OF ILLINOIS

ILLINOIS STATE HOUSE, VANDALIA.

THE LIBRARY
OF THE
UNIVERSITY OF ILLINOIS

ILLINOIS STATE HOUSE, KASKASKIA.

THE LIBRARY
OF THE
UNIVERSITY OF ILLINOIS

WOMAN'S EXHIBIT.

THE LIBRARY
OF THE
UNIVERSITY OF ILLINOIS

THE ILLINOIS WOMAN'S EXPOSITION BOARD

AT THE WORLD'S COLUMBIAN EXPOSITION.

President, - - Mrs. Marcia Louise Gould, Moline.
Vice-President, - Mrs. Robert H. Wiles, Freeport.
Secretary, - Miss Mary Callahan, Robinson.

BOARD OF DIRECTORS:

Mrs. Richard J. Oglesby, - - - - Moline.
Mrs. Frances L. Gilbert, - - Chicago.
Mrs. Francine E. Patton, - - Springfield.
Mrs. Isabella Laning Candee, - - Cairo.
Mrs. Frances Welles Shepard, - - - Chicago.

The Illinois Woman's Exposition Board was organized by act of the Legislature "to represent the industries of the women of Illinois at the World's Columbian Exposition." To enable it to successfully execute the duty thus assigned to it, $80,000, or one-tenth of the total State appropriation, was placed at its disposal in the State Treasury. The appointment for the first time of a State Board composed entirely of women and the conferring upon it of such large financial responsibilities, limited in no way except by its own sense of expediency and right, marks a most significant advance in the public recognition of woman's business ability and capacity for affairs. In view of this fact the Board believes that it may without undue pride call the attention of the people whom it (jointly with the Illinois Board of World's Fair Commissioners) represents, not only to its work as installed at the Columbian Exposition, but also to its history during the past two years of its official existence. The history of the Board is the history of its accomplished work alone. The public press of the State and especially of the city of Chicago, which has given the board most generous and appreciative notice and has reported the plans of the board for representing the industries and interests of Illinois women and the realization of such plans in the installation of exhibits. As the result of this installation, there are in active daily operation at Jackson Park a hospital, a pharmacy, a kitchen and a kindergarten, conducted entirely by women, and also an exhibit of material objects representing as fully as possible the results of woman's industry in the home, the factory, the studio and the professions.

In the Illinois Woman's Hospital, situated southwest of the Children's Building, men, women and children receive, free of charge, the services of women surgeons, physicians and trained nurses of one of three schools of medicine, allopathic, homœopathic or eclectic.

In the pharmacy State registered women pharmacists compound and dispense drugs and fill prescriptions.

In the kitchen which is the contribution of Illinois women to the Woman's Building, practical demonstration lessons are given each morning upon the proper cooking of maize or Indian corn, one of the staple products of Illinois, and yet one whose nutritive value and palatable preparation are little understood either at home or abroad. In the afternoon, cooking lessons not restricted to Indian corn are given to a class of girls, illustrating how cooking may be taught in industrial or trade schools. Because of lack of sufficient space this hospital, pharmacy and kitchen are located outside of the Illinois Building, but the kindergarten and all other exhibits hereinafter described are found in the Illinois Building.

During the first three months of the Exposition, the kindergarten was conducted by the Froebel Kindergarten Association of Chicago. During the months of August, September and October, it is conducted by the Free Kindergarten Association of the same city. The sessions are held every morning except Saturday from 9 until 12 o'clock, and visitors are cordially invited, in order that the personal knowledge of their philanthropic and most valuable educational system may spread to every village in the State. The kindergarten room itself is a model of beauty and convenience, and, with the grand outlook from the windows and the happy childhood within, is a sight never to be forgotten.

In attempting to gather together the material results of woman's handicraft, the Board has earnestly striven to represent all classes of industry, and so far as possible, every locality in the State. Merit alone has been the test, and all objects placed upon exhibition have successfully passed the judgment of juries of experts.

As a matter of practical expediency in collecting and planning for exhibits, the different members of the Board were assigned to the chairmanship of the following committee:

Literature, including books, newspapers and magazines.

Educational, philanthropic and professional work.

Historical and scientific exhibit.

Fine arts, including sculpture, painting in oil and water colors, chalk, charcoal, pastel and other drawings.

Decorative art, including ceramics, leather work, pyrography, wood carving and plain and ornamental needlework.

Practical arts, including photographs, book illustrations, designs, inventions and manufactures.

Domestic science, including kitchen and pantry stores.

All these different lines of activity are represented in the exhibit, although in many cases only a few examples of the best work of each kind could be shown because of the limited space, 42x150 feet, at the disposal of the board. For the same reason the showing of many industries on a more elaborate scale and with fuller detail was prohibited.

In literature, five hundred books written by women, residents in Illinois, thirteen magazines and twenty-seven newspapers edited by them were gathered together, and housed in a library, designed and decorated in the early renaissance style by Illinois women. Of the authors thus represented, one is a member of the Philosophical Society of London and of the International Congress of Orientalists and another of the National American

Geographical Society, and among them is the editor and proprietor of the official court journal of the State of Illinois, "The Chicago Legal News."

The educational, philanthropic and professional work was necessarily shown in great part by means of statistics. These statistics are displayed in a large, hand-engrossed, bound book made entirely by women, and are also printed in pamphlet form for distribution. It is not claimed that these statistics by any means cover the ground, as a complete work of the kind would have required the labor of many individuals for many months, but it is believed that they are a valuable addition to present knowledge and are full of significant hints to the student of history and of political economy.

Students of history will also find much that is interesting in the relics exhibited pertaining to the early history of Illinois, and to the lives of its great heroes in later days, Lincoln and Grant. We have the portraits of the first governor of Illinois, Shadrach Bond, and of his wife, and many articles of furniture and household adornment from Old Kaskaskia, the first capitol city of Illinois and, most memorable of all, the first church bell rung west of the Alleghenies, a bell presented by the king of France to the Mission of Kaskaskia in 1742. There are portraits of Grant and Lincoln and a large number of personal relics. In the historical exhibit are also many unique articles illustrating the handicraft of the pioneer women of Illinois. Space forbids their enumeration here, and also that of hundreds of special articles exhibited in other departments and the interested reader is for anything like a full account referred to the official catalogue of the Illinois Woman's Exposition Board.

In science, an active exhibit in bacteriological laboratory work is made by an instructor in one of our leading universities. In entomology, scientific drawings are shown which challenge comparison with the best work of the kind. Taxidermy, botany (including marine algae), and geology are also represented.

In sculpture, the visitor is greeted by an ideal female figure, "Illinois Welcoming the Nations of the World." Other statues adorn the walls. There are a large number of carefully selected paintings and drawings, several of which have won high praise from artists of acknowledged ability. The frieze in the reception room illustrates the relation of women to the arts, and was painted in panels by ten Illinois woman artists. Worthy of notice in this room, also, is a cabinet of miniatures painted on ivory by one exhibitor. Among the artists are nine who have obtained the distinction of exhibiting in the Paris salon. A large part of the fine arts exhibit was received from the Palette Club of Chicago.

In ceramics there are almost 200 different specimens of work, many in wood carving, several in embossed and illuminated leather work, tables and chairs in pyrogravure (poker work in old-fashioned parlance) and a large collection of needle work of all kinds, showing how woman with her needle supplies many of the necessities of life and also contributes to the decorative beauty of her surroundings. The ecclesiastical embroideries and those of the Chicago Decorative Art Society especially attract the surprised attention of visitors. Much decorative work is shown as an object lesson in the woman's reception room, such as modelling, carving, designing and weaving, the entire room being to a large extent an exhibit of woman's work.

The department of photography is made notable by one exhibitor who obtained a diploma for distinguished excellence at the Vienna Exhibition in 1891. Another exhibitor shows carbon prints on porcelain. Book illustrations, and designs crowd the space allotted to them. Two hundred and forty-nine inventions are shown ranging in character from sewing, cooking and nursing appliances, pertaining especially to the employment of women, to harvesters, harness attachments, car couplers, hay presses and other implements or processes for use in occupations in which women are seldom engaged.

Manufactures are shown by finished products from factories owned and managed entirely by women, and also by a series of one hundred and eight photographs showing women at work with men in the factories, where the finished products are the result of their combined labor.

Woman's skill in the preserving and canning of fruit and the making of jelly is shown by choice examples.

The silk industry is exhibited from the beginning in the egg to the woven silk fabric.

The women farmers of the State show grain inferior to none even in the great Agricultural Building.

Scientific reproductions of fruit and vegetables are shown in wax.

The Woman's Relief Corps of the State has decorated the ceiling of the exhibit space with its flags and banners, and also displays the rosters of the different corps of the State.

There are several memorial volumes showing research in history and skill in the decorative making of books, as well as containing tributes to woman's industry and ability in many practical directions, not capable of material representation.

Throughout the whole exhibit of the industries of the women of Illinois, thus most cursorily outlined, the aim of the Illinois Woman's Exposition Board has been to show, first, the excellence of the work of every kind done by Illinois women; second, the best methods and the best results in the every-day affairs of life; third, the new avenues constantly opening by which woman may earn her livelihood or add to the sum of human happiness and wisdom.

www.ingramcontent.com/pod-product-compliance
Lightning Source LLC
Chambersburg PA
CBHW022123160426
43197CB00009B/1131